THE JOY OF
DYSFUNCTIONAL
FAMILIES

David Walton Earle, LPC

Books
What To Do While You Count To 10
Professor of Pain
Iron Mask
Red Roses 'n Pinstripes
Love Is Not Enough
Gilligan's Notes
Simple Communication for Complicated People
Contents of a Small Boy's Pocket
Recovery Stories

Twelve Steps workbooks:
Wisdom of the Steps – 1st Step
Wisdom of the Steps – 2nd Step
Wisdom of the Steps – 3rd Step
Wisdom of the Steps – 1st, 2nd, and 3rd Steps (combined)
Wisdom of the Steps – 4th Step
Wisdom of the Steps – 5th Step
Wisdom of the Steps – 6th Step

Co-authored
Leadership – Helping Others to Succeed
Senator George Mitchell, Patricia Schroeder, et al

Extreme Excellence
Michael Higson, Arlene R. Taylor, et al

You Might Need a Therapist If...
Cliff Carle, John Carfi

THE JOY OF DYSFUNCTIONAL FAMILIES

Joke Book

DAVID WALTON EARLE, LPC

Copyright © 2019 David Walton Earle, LPC

Cover Designed and Cartoons by Cover Judith Gusse

All rights reserved. No part of this publication may be reproduced or transmitted, in any form or by any means, electronic, mechanical, photocopying, recorded, or otherwise, without the prior written permission of the author.

ISBN-13:978-1726337342
ISBN-10: 1726337340

Barleywood Publishing
Baton Rouge, LA
Printed by CreateSpace

"What is learned through play is learned to stay."
- Anonymous

"All parents damage their children. It cannot be helped. Youth, like pristine glass, absorbs the prints of its handlers. Some parents smudge, others crack, a few shatter childhoods completely into jagged pieces, beyond repair."

—Mitch Albom

Table of Contents

Introducing Chaos ix

Smile Statements xiii

Halt xvii

Joy-Robbing Habits xix

Chapter 1. Evasive Joy Robbers 1

Chapter 2. Soul Wounded Joy Robbers 13

Chapter 3. Disconnected Joy Robbers 29

Chapter 4. Command/Control Joy Robbers 43

Chapter 5. Low Self-Worth Joy Robbers 55

Appendix 73

Suggested Reading 93

About the Author 95

Acknowledgement 99

Introducing Chaos

Most people grew up in dysfunctional households – often damaged by well-intentioned parents. Some children experienced a little dysfunction, and some quite a lot. Many other writers seek to enlighten readers about childhood emotional wounds, and provide understanding and acceptance of them. *The Joy of Dysfunctional Families* seeks the same but with an added invitation to accept whatever characteristic dysfunction you currently "enjoy" and not to take yourself so seriously. Yes, you may have experienced pain and discomfort growing up when you did not receive what a child needs for proper development. Despite your history, do you have to give away your joy? What keeps you from seeing the absurdities in your life? Can you change your history by being stern? Why can't you laugh? Even with your suffering, *The Joy of Dysfunctional Families* seeks to put the "fun" back into dysfunction!

Both my dog, Fletcher, and cat, Hobbes, were rescue animals, so I did not meet their parents nor have the opportunity to discuss their home environment, pedigree, or family history with the adoption agency. If the agency knew of their family background, they did not pass it on. Having lived with these animals for many years and with my training as a substance abuse counselor, I am convinced that they both *were adult children of alcoholics!*

I know this to be true for I witnessed the result of their less-than-perfect parents. The recovering community often explains living with alcoholics with a tongue-in-cheek reality, "Alcoholics do not have relationships – **they take hostages!**" This does not mean alcoholics are necessarily bad people, but it is hard to love someone or be loved by someone so afflicted with this destructive disease.

My two pets had many of the characteristics of Adult Children of Alcoholics (or more realistically, Adult Children of Dysfunctional Families). They were very needy, controlling, demanding, fearful, and very unhappy – sad eyes. When compared to other animals, what was so striking was their complete and total lack of joy – *they did not know how to play!* What cat doesn't play with string or stalk imaginary prey, pouncing upon their victim with joyful glee of victory? What dog doesn't want to chase a ball or run uninhibited with a slobbery tongue, full of joy? Not mine.

I tried to get these animals to attend a Twelve-Steps meeting of Adult Children of Alcoholics. One time, Fletcher actually attended a meeting – one meeting. After the meeting, he looked at me with those big eyes, jumped on me with extreme excitement he had never shown before or after, and barked, "This is my meeting, I loved it. They understand me!" To him, this must have seemed like a place of healing – where others accepted him as he was – character flaws and all – a place, through honesty, where he could retrieve the happiness he had so long ago given away. As excited as he was with that one meeting, sadly, he *never* returned to "his meeting." I never understood his reluctance. I guess change is so hard – he would not allow his pain to overcome his resistance to change.

Life can only be understood backwards,
but it must be lived forwards."
—Soren Kierkgaard

The cat would not hear of attending. He told me he was too smart to "... sit around with a bunch of unhappy people and talk about problems." Once I tried to get my cat to attend counseling, "I'll pay for it," I offered. He told me that he "...was too intelligent for counseling."

They both were stuck in misery, unwilling to think any of the world's happiness could be theirs, determined to never allow joy into their self-imposed darkness. Sometimes, when I did a little dance trying to cheer Hobbs up, he would look at me with all the distain only a cat could muster and say, "...quit blowing sunshine up my butt."

Over the years, both turned out to be good friends, but it saddened me to live with deniers of joy. Many of us desperately want to be happy and have a safe place of acceptance – some find it in the accepting confines of a Twelve-Step fellowship. Others, like my pets, choose not to explore themselves to the degree of honesty recovery requires.

My animals were exactly as described – well, maybe without the conversations, but they had traits so common to sufferers from dysfunctional families. I used the example of my talking animals to exaggerate a point. Often, our understanding increases when viewing a truth from an enlarged and preposterous point of view. From my own personal experience, I understand many of these misery-invoking traits from when I dragged my family through my own unhappiness.

In this book, *The Joy of Dysfunctional Families* – we are able to poke fun at our vulnerability and character flaws. In this self-help joke book, we learn through absurdity. Here we get to laugh at what is so unlaughable. Humor also lets us explore very uncomfortable thoughts and memories.

> "The *shortest distance between two people is a laugh.*"
>
> —Victor Borge

Smile Statements

In this book are several smile statements after each dysfunctional character trait. It is suggested you first read the characteristic and understand the dysfunctional trait first, then read the smile statement knowing your face will record a facial expression. Maybe, I hope, it will be a smile coming from humor – real side splitters, after all this is a JOKE book. Then again, your smile may be from an ironic point of view. This awareness allows us to look inward and not take ourselves so seriously. Irony often uncovers the realities of the truth. Acknowledge your chaos, then sit back, let it go, embrace your dysfunction – it belongs to you and by now, is your long well-known traveling companion. You already paid a large price for these coping skills, but now they are your ticket to change. With this pass – that you already bought - you get to travel inward laughing at yourself, sometimes in pain but mostly in joy.

Some of your smiles may come from new understanding. Perhaps, your smile may be the bewilderment of how this one-liner ever made it in the covers of a "joke" book. I hope those disappointments are very rare.

These characteristic traits are similar to what three self-help organizations conclude: Adult Children of Alcoholics, Codependent Anonymous, and Al Anon (see Appendix). Reading these traits, you may too identify with the painful realities of your current or past coping skills. These characteristics are not the exclusive property of Adult Children of Alcoholics or codependents, but unfortunately, are common to many people - even those not raised in an alcoholic home. A better description should be *adult children of dysfunctional parents*; for even without the disease of alcoholism, dysfunction occurs in all homes. Your level may be different from others, but unless you are a saint or had perfect parents, you will relate to some of these joy-robbing habits.

As you watch sitcoms on TV, watch for these dysfunctional characteristics as comedians depict this behavior in exaggerated forms, allowing us to laugh at their antics. On a deeper lever, as we watch sitcoms, we experience our own absurdities and find it much easier and less painful to laugh than cry. Perhaps laughing at these shows is a form of hiding that we engage in to protect what we do not wish to acknowledge openly – called denial.

Most people suffered from imperfect parenting but what if your parents were perfect? Would perfect parents be a form of child abuse? Perfect parents would set up their offspring to expect something not available in the real world! Even with the less-than-perfect parents you were blessed with, you can still enjoy the wisdom in this book. In fact, if your parents had not passed their dysfunction on to you, how could not see any humor in the one-liners? Maybe through the pain of your youth and the reality of today, you can contrast them together with humor. With this understanding and with your tongue *firmly* embedded in your cheek, you can thank your parents for all the wonderful and entertaining dysfunction you experienced growing up! Think of all the breathtaking opportunities you now have of laughing at yourself. Thanks, Mom. Thanks, Dad.

The key question is, do you allow your dysfunctional coping skills to control you? Do you have to allow past wounds of what you needed, but did not receive, dictate your joy today? By acknowledging your *joy robbers,* this allows you to take back the power you gave away and instead ... *laugh!*

> *"It is never too late to have a happy childhood."*
> —Claudia Black

You have wounds from your past. You also have wounds from your present. Perhaps, you realize that your current coping skills are highly suspect ... in fact, maybe some *just plain suck.* Oh well, welcome to the human race! With your personal private brand of dysfunction, you can now laugh heartily as you just might see yourself in this book. After your laughter dies down and the reality of your pain is out in the open, you may wish to change to a more effective way of living. I promise you smiles on your journey through these pages. At the end of the book in the Appendix are many more dysfunctional coping skills. Recognize your character defects and decide if they are working for you and if not, then make a decision if you want to change or not.

As a literary composition, *The Joy of Dysfunctional Families* has its own brand of dysfunction. This book cannot decide if it is a joke book or not. Maybe it is a self-help book with deep and profound realizations awaiting the reader's discovery or maybe just a joke book with limited value and easy to forget. . Regardless of how you view this book - most people even with different intelligence, interests, backgrounds, and learning styles - can increase their thinking ability especially in an enjoyable learning environment. Humor can reduce anxiety, boost participation, and increase motivation, allowing the reader to explore difficult and painful experiences. ***Humor is misery's antidote!*** Through humor, you'll find *The Joy of Dysfunctional Families* a lighthearted way of thinking about serious problems through self-reflection. I hope you enjoy reading it as much as I enjoyed writing it.

**Shall we explore our dysfunctions
and laugh together?**

Halt

Many of us had to grow up too quickly and as a result, and like my dog and cat, you have difficulty having fun. You tend to take yourself too seriously, and it is hard for you to let down our hair and just enjoy life. For example, in the Alcoholics Anonymous fellowship, many refer to the acronym H.A.L.T. when describing the most significant times when an alcoholic is more vulnerable to relapse.

H – Hungry   **A** - Angry   **L** – Lonely   **T** – Tired

When addicts find themselves in one or more of these conditions – especially in their tender sobriety - the acronym HALT indicates caution. This awareness serves a much-needed warning, but HALT, by itself, left something important out. It should be HALTS. In this version, the *S* stands for *serious*. When alcoholics - or anyone for that matter - gets too serious, dysfunctional behavior is more likely.

You may identify with some of the various dysfunctional characteristics called *Joy-Robbers*. You either have one or more traits or know others who exhibit this behavior. Knowing what they are provides you the opportunity to change your behavior. Question: just because we decided to work on a character defect does it mean we have to be so serious? Can we not look at ourselves, and despite our personal Joy Robbers, laugh at ourselves?

Read the Joy Robbers Habits, take the personal profile, and then, enjoy the following one-liners. Give yourself permission to laugh. STOP. Don't skip the personal profile. STOP. It may be hard and something you may not be comfortable doing **BUT** give yourself permission to explore yourself. Feel the emotion expense incurred by this Joy Robbers then laugh – spit in the eye of your pain and laugh – your humor will help you to change.

Now consider making a conscious decision to experience joy. Momentarily, discard your stuffy adult attitude and look at these one-liners with the eyes of someone who really wants to laugh – who loves to giggle. Laugh hardy, laugh often; put a big "S" into your personal HALTS.

Joy-Robbing Habits

Before you enjoy the anticipated humor, read each chapter's list of Joy-Robbing traits. Take the profile by rating yourself from one to five, with five being the highest.

This way you'll understand the trait from a personal point of view. This connection will increase this book's enjoyment and your learning.

WANTED
DEAD OR ALIVE

EVASIVE

JOY ROBBER

Description: Attaches to things to avoid close relationships, beats around the bush when communicating, fears being vulnerable so is detached from expressing feelings, craves intimacy but hides from vulnerable, has difficulty expressing gratitude.

CHAPTER ONE

EVASIVE JOY ROBBERS

Give yourself a score of 1-5 depending on your identity to the trait with 5 being the most.

I harshly judge others.	
I avoid intimacy to maintain distance	
I allow my addictive behavior to limit intimacy.	
I use evasive communication to avoid conflict	
I keep my feelings to myself	
I want intimacy but push others away when I receive it (push-pull effect).	
Strong people do not express personal feelings.	

Strong people do not express personal feelings.

"Emotions?" Is there an app for that?

You can handle any pain, that is... until it hurts.

In the jail between your ears ... you cannot cry.

Under your chest, your dead soul has no feelings.

You have yet to learn - your ego is not to be your amigo.

The rock concert in your head keeps your emotions away.

Introspection is scary. What if you searched inside yourself and found nothing there?

I judge others harshly.

You never go to bed mad but instead stay awake plotting revenge.

You vow never to come out your room because your wife is acting so childish.

Your expectations are only resentments under construction.

You love the human race – it is the people you cannot stand.

Your last family reunion reminded you of central booking.

You are not afraid of Satan, you've married to Lucifer's sister.

I judge others harshly - continued.

Since you have no sin, you are entitled to throw stones.

You do not mingle with your peers, since you have no peers.

Your best attempt at expressing deep love often comes out as ... *Nazi Nurturing.*

It's so hard to be humble with all your magnificence.

I avoid intimacy to maintain distance.

You had to cancel your second childhood for lack of adult supervision

You wanted a mate just like mom, and you finally found her in the line to the complaint department.

You think marriage gives you a license to irritate a special person for life.

Your mother taught you not to get angry – just be nice.

You accomplished your lifetime goal – finding someone sick enough to marry you.

You married for better or worse. He couldn't do much better – you couldn't do much worse.

You used your jail experience to provide a greater opportunity for male bonding.

I allow my addictive behavior to limit intimacy.

You checked yourself into the Hokey Pokey Clinic ... you know ... *to turn yourself around*

Self-reliant failed you.

Your struggle did not free you from life's quicksand.

Your attitude of "it's all-about-me" got you here in the first place.

You think your bad day can always be improved with a drink.

You saw your teacher featured in a porn movie. You were homeschooled.

You tried to bribe the monkey to get off your back.

Drinking increases your quotient of awesomeness.

You have tennis elbow from compulsive masturbation.

With the addition of alcohol, you turn into an instant asshole.

You were sober for over 15 years then you had your 16th birthday.

You found the little bottles are much easier to hide.

You keep searching for the perfect day to relapse.

I allow my addictive behavior to limit intimacy -continued.

It is as difficult to hide all your secrets as it is to hold balloons under the water.

You wanted to want to quit, but your quitter did not want to quit.

Your friends think you have the personality of an assassin.

Alcohol compliments your hemorrhoids creating a perfect asshole.

I use evasive communication to avoid conflict.

You get off to the wrong foot simply by shoving it into your mouth.

Your best conflict resolution skill is straddling contradictions.

You haven't spoken to your wife in two weeks and don't intend on interrupting her.

Other people think you talk too much, but it is not that you're excessively verbal but you're deadly afraid of silence.

You say one thing but really mean your mother.

You enjoy a good debate but love screaming obscenities more.

You don't lie. You just tell the truth with bad intentions.

You are excellent in attentive ignoring.

You know all the answers, but *no one asks you.*

I keep my feelings to myself.

When you dialed your current reality ... it was no longer in service.

Every time you hear a pop-top open, you are nine years old again.

You wake up grouchy, and for the rest of the day, it's all downhill.

The only way you can feel better about yourself is to be with someone worse than you.

When someone says, "Have a Great Day," you have other plans.

Your boyfriend gets lonely sleeping with you.

It is only your passionate hatred giving your life meaning.

I keep my feelings to myself - continued.

Getting dressed for you is deciding what style mask to hide behind.

I want intimacy but push others away when I receive it (*push-pull* effect).

You burn bridges you need to cross and repair ones needing destruction.

Your ex sent you a card: "I'm so miserable without you, it's almost like you're still here."

You tried to bribe the judge to lift the restraining order so you could date your ex-girlfriend.

I want intimacy but push others away when I receive it (*push-pull effect*) - continued.

You believe eye contact is an act of aggression.

You are pleased to see your boyfriend arrive but never sorry when he leaves.

The only control you know is out-of-control.

Your horniness is the essence of your quintessential definition of hope despite all past experiences.

Your mother sends her love but you don't believe her.

Thumb Work

What is the difference between pointing your finger at someone else - putting your focus on them, or when you bend your elbows - pointing your thumbs directly at yourself? Hint: If you wish to achieve happiness, pointing your finger at others or bending your elbow toward yourself makes all the difference in world.

You were raised in chaos where you learned certain behaviors that can steal joy from any family. These dysfunctional habits became *Joy Robbers* - the exchange medium of your family. Reading the list of Joy Robbers, you can easily see what character defects you inherited – what you needed, but did not receive. Each chapter has a list of these destructive habits – these *Joy Robbers,* your inheritance - where many continue to this day. The truth is, everyone was raised in chaos – some more than others. Once acknowledged, they now belong to you. Like it or not, they are yours. It matters not where or why you developed your *Joy-Robbing* habits, the key question is what you are going to do about it.

Pointing your finger at your family or another person and blaming them for your misery creates its own gravitational pull, reinforcing the problems you now face. Pointing your finger at another is an excellent way of avoiding the responsibility – the glue holding your unhappiness in place. Blaming your family only sticks you deeper in Tar Baby's trap. Accept that your parents were not perfect, had their own hurts and wounds, but probably raised you the best they knew how.

The opposite of finger pointing is *Thumb Work*. Bend your elbows and point your thumbs at yourself – be responsible. Although *Thumb Work* is uncomfortable and often painful, it is the antidote to your collection of Joy Robbers. This is your key to the happiness and joy – that inner peace you so longed for, wished for, and now know that through *Thumb Work*, it can be yours.

My Life Will Change ...
When I Change!

Mother to her grown daughter, *"Dear, if all your problems were created by how you were raised, guess what. Today they are all yours!"*

WANTED

DEAD OR ALIVE

SOUL-WOUNDING

JOY ROBBER

Description: Goes along to get along, confuses sex with love, will lie to gain appreciation from others, overly sensitive to the feeling of others, walks on eggshells to avoid conflict, and willing to compromise values to gain acceptance.

CHAPTER TWO

SOUL WOUNDED JOY ROBBERS

Give yourself a score of 1-5 depending on your identity to the trait with 5 being the most.

Regardless of the consequences, I am very loyal.	
I allow anger and fear of rejection to control me.	
Other people's desires are more important than mine.	
I live my life as a victim.	
I take on the feelings of others.	
I am afraid to express myself when I differ with others.	
It's difficult for me to "let go" and have fun.	
I confuse sexual attention and love.	
I love people I can pity and rescue.	
A potential consequence seldom alters my decisions.	
I am addicted to excitement.	
My values are less important than other's approval.	

Regardless of the consequences, I am very loyal.

Attending your family reunion is like returning to the scene of the crime.

Your only attachment to your significant other is through the checkbook.

You'd like to lose weight, but now your fat is the only friend you have.

The battered women's shelter is on your speed dial.

The honeymoon part of the abuse cycle is worth all the pain he can inflict.

You continue to fill your sick abandonment needs with someone who left three years ago.

After you got out of a bad roller coaster relationship – you bought another ticket.

You now know the truth, but you still believe her lies.

You base your entire outlook on life on people you like the least.

You translated "...*turn the other cheek* ..." into a one-sided face-slapping contest.

> "It's hard to see red flags if you are wearing rose-colored glasses."
> —BoJack Hoseman

I allow anger and fear of rejection to control me.

> You are a great reservoir for everyone's shame and blame.
>
> Your great resolve to say "no" dissolved into "Why yes, I'd love to."
>
> When Jeffery Dahmer invited you to dinner... you accepted.
>
> Getting down on yourself is an art form.
>
> Your goals are so low; you achieve the perfect score of *10* for your plunging status quo.
>
> You allow your wife to choose what kind of day you are having.

Other people's desires are more important than mine.

> When you wallowed with the pigs, you were surprised when you got dirty.
>
> The closest thing to intimacy you ever experienced is spelling the word at your 3rd grade spelling bee.
>
> Your perfect man comes with a warning label.
>
> You socialize with everyone else because you don't want to be alone with you.
>
> Drinking wine out of your sippy cup satisfies both your inner child and your emerging sophistication.
>
> You had a panic attack the one time you did what you wanted.

I live my life as a victim.

The only reason you married the boy next store was because you were never allowed to cross the street.

You would like to be yourself, but when you do, someone else always causes you to fail.

You wanted to set the world on fire, but they took your matches away.

You received *Sufferer of the Year* award in recognition for excelling at being the victim.

You blamed the rage you inflicted on your daughter on what you experienced growing up.

When you played possum, the vultures ate you.

For the last 30 years on life's highway, you have been in a construction zone.

They call you Barbie – all plastic and no brains.

You get your gratitude by reading the daily obits.

All your bad luck came from when you entered a fiddle contest for the golden fiddle ... and lost.

I live my life as a victim - continued.

When life asks, "Who wants to be a victim?"
You jump up yelling, *"Choose me, Choose me!"*

I take on the feelings of others.

You look so care-worn you make Abraham Lincoln look happy.

You divorced your spouse just to get him to show some emotions.

After sex, you ask, "Was that good for you? How was it for me?"

You are thankful of your diagnosis of antisocial personality, at least they can no longer call you an asshole.

Numbness is the closest you get to a state of grace.

I am afraid to express myself when I differ with others.

When you argue with yourself and are so incensed, you cop an attitude and stomp away.

When you hit the Control Alt Delete button on your Computer – *you disappeared.*

You can change your personality faster than Superman in a phone booth.

You are drowning, and someone else's life flashes before your eyes.

You see yourself as a doormat but are surprised then they wipe their muddy feet on you.

You're not a pessimist just a cured optimist.

When you have brainstorms, others think it a very light drizzles.

It difficult for me to "let go", have fun.

You spell fun without the "u."

To others you are an euphoric inhibitor.

To accomplish spontaneity, you have to include it on your to-do list.

You trade feelings of joy for the bitter bile of resentment.

It difficult for me to "let go", have fun - continued.

Your life is like a piece of Swiss cheese – much missing and the rest stinks.

You wake up next to a chewed-off arm.

You invited your friends to your tenth annual divorce party.

You are sure that if the world didn't suck you'd fall off.

You had fun once but did not enjoy it.

You dropped your key to happiness
down the drain of suffering.

I confuse sexual attention and love.

You got married to change him into the father you never had.

I confuse sexual attention and love - continued.

Your definition of intimacy is when the prostitute doesn't immediately leave.

Your knight-in-shining-armor turned out to be a jerk clad in aluminum foil.

You meet a cute guy who has just been released from prison as a axe murderer. You ask him, "So, you're single?"

Your magnetic personality only attracts stray cats and needy boyfriends.

When you make nineteen or twenty mistakes, people consider you a tramp.

With every boy you meet, your imagination goes from "nice buns," to heart flutter, to enduring love, and then visions of matrimony; all in the time it takes to write your phone number.

You meet someone new you think, "Is this the man I want my kids to spend every other weekend with?"

Your best description of your love life is between a *sock* and a hard place.

I confuse sexual attention and love - continued.

You stood at the altar saying, "I do," with your hand behind your back and your fingers crossed

I love people I can pity and rescue.

You know one hundred and one ways to make love ... but have no girlfriend.

Every time you had a romance, your wife always interfered.

After your first date, you realize you need the protection of a full-body condom. You then made another date.

You couldn't communicate with your boyfriend so you married him.

If you think that the fastest way to a man's bedroom is through his kitchen, you failed geography.

A potential consequence seldom alters my decisions.

It is not that you are stupid, but you have terrible luck with thinking.

You explain your tendency for making the same mistake again and again as, "Some mistakes are just too damn fun not to repeat."

Instead of coming out of the subway of denial, you dug more tunnels.

You listen to the tar baby in your head.

Your attention span is the size of a quarter. It hasn't improved since you gave out change.

You gave up wise contemplation for Lent.

Once you let your mind wander, but it never came back.

Your God has a sloped forehead. Every time you repeat the same mistake, he slaps his forehead and says, "Ahh, he did it again!"

You let others take your advice since you never use it.

I am addicted to excitement.

Your reward for *Messing with Texas* was a shotgun wedding.

You do everything by the process of elimination, starting with the worst decisions and working your way toward the best.

I am addicted to excitement - continued.

You make someone who has *Attention Deficit/Hyperactivity Disorder* appear to be standing still.

You are a kleptomaniac. When life gets bad - you take something for it.

You are more tenacious than a Jehovah's Witness with an Amway franchise.

Your flowerbeds are in the shape of crime scene chalk outlines.

Your head is a scary place to be.

Today, you skydived from 20,000 feet, climbed the Matterhorn, and then called your mother to tell her not to worry.

Your goal in life is to be shot by a jealous husband at the age of 87.

You know you do not have a problem since you never drank alone – you always had your dog.

My values are less important than other's approval.

Your veracity often plays peek-a-boo with the truth.

Your carefully crafted image came apart when the Wizard of Oz wanted his curtain back.

My values are less important than other's approval - continued.

You cut your conscious to fit the fashion of the day.

It was frightening when you got lost in thought - it was such unfamiliar territory.

You now consider yourself well informed - your wife just told you what she thinks of you.

The only time you are comfortable being yourself is when you are on stage acting out someone else's life.

Best Education

People in recovery, working a Twelve-Step Program, often do not know the full magnitude of the resource they now have. If you wanted to study human nature, experience the inspiration of overcoming all odds, and learn how to live a more profound and peaceful life, then welcome to recovery. When in those rooms with like-minded individuals - all dedicated to changing themselves - something magical happens.

A Twelve-Step program is the best education money cannot buy! This education costs no monetary amount but does require a lifetime to learn. If you want peace - if you want serenity, then sit on the folding chairs set out in the classroom of recovery. With your addiction and/or codependency, you have already paid the tuition. You earned it through all the pain and misery you experienced, all the damage you inflicted upon others, and all the regret of the joy you gave away. Recovery is a beautiful, beyond-all-expectations place, however, this transitional education does require work – often painful work – but the rewards are immeasurable.

Recovery Promises

We are going to know a new freedom and a new happiness. We will not regret the past nor wish to shut the door on it. We will comprehend the word serenity, and we will know peace. No matter how far down the scale we have gone, we will see how our experience can benefit others. That feeling of uselessness and self-pity will disappear. We will lose interest in selfish things and gain interest in our fellows. Self-seeking will slip away. Our whole attitude and outlook on life will change. Fear of people and economic insecurity will leave us. We will intuitively know how to handle situations which used to baffle us. We will suddenly realize that god is doing for us what we could not do for ourselves.

This excerpt from the *Alcoholics Anonymous* (3rd Edition), pages 83-84, is reprinted with permission of Alcoholics Anonymous World Services, Inc (A.A.W.S.). Permission to use this excerpt does not mean that A.A.W.S. is in any way affiliated with this program. A.A. is a program of recovery from alcoholism only – use of this material in connection with programs and activities which are patterned after A.A., but which address other problems or concerns, or in any other non-A.A. context, does not imply otherwise.

Can any other education offer those promises? I think not. Keep coming back. As they say in the meetings, "It works *if YOU work it.*"

WANTED
DEAD OR ALIVE

DISCONNECTED

JOY ROBBER

Description: Very detached, often depressed, lonely, difficulty with identifying and expressing feelings, refuses help especially when needed, and is excellent at masking personal pain.

CHAPTER THREE

DISCONNECTED JOY ROBBERS

Give yourself a score of 1-5 depending on your identity to the trait with 5 being the most.

I am not connected to my emotions.	
I deny or minimize what my emotions tell me.	
I am totally focused on the well-being of others.	
Others' feelings are unimportant to me.	
I have an inflated sense of self-worth and self-importance.	
I mask my pain in various ways such as anger, humor, or isolation.	
I express negativity or aggression in indirect and passive ways.	
I frighten people with my anger and belittling criticism.	
I am attracted to the unavailability of others.	
I have difficulty attracting or maintaining intimate relationships.	
I abandon others before they can abandon me.	
I need a compulsive personality, such as a workaholic, alcoholic, etc. to fill my sick abandonment needs.	
I am terrified of abandonment and will do anything to hold on to a relationship.	

I am not connected to my emotions.

You reconcile your bad luck with all the bad karma you have left to burn off.

You got kicked out of the airport for leaving your emotional baggage unattended.

You have to dial long distance to reach your emotions.

You treat your emotions like children, rather than let them drive, you strap them in the back seat and let them cry themselves to sleep.

Even with your emotional immaturity, you know when she points a gun at you she probably has not forgiven you.

You love your wife so much - you really do - so much in fact, you almost told her.

You are too afraid to admit your fears.

I deny or minimize what my emotions tell me.

With your friends ... who needs hallucinations?

You gave up on finding yourself, instead joined the hunt for Waldo.

You are good at faking orgasms; hell, you can fake the whole relationship.

Your clear conscience comes from a bad memory.

I deny or minimize what my emotions tell me - continued.

Your mind is so open people can feel a breeze.

You apologize for coughing when someone blows smoke in your face.

You think – therefore you worry.

You now know you cannot win a spiritual war without a spirit.

You have perfected the zombie perfect state of numbness.

I am totally focused on the well-being of others.

You are like a drink on the house, and no one goes home thirsty.

You never say, "Now I'll do what is best for me."

You were so focused on others you forgot your own funeral.

They call you "Caterpillar" – the only way you can keep your relationship is by crawling.

You are the travel agent for guilt trips.

You would feel terribly vulnerable if you did not feel guilty.

Your nickname is "wags." Like a dog, you try to please everyone.

Other's feelings are unimportant to me.

You are not a bad listener – you just don't give a damn.

You were so busy getting the speck out of his eye you did not see the log in yours.

At puberty, you said goodbye to your boyhood and looked forward to adultery.

You finally found your one true love but then discovered you can't marry yourself.

In any conversation, you are *me-deep* in discussion.

You define anyone who tries to borrow money from you as an optimist.

You think a cheap shot is a terrible thing to waste.

I have an inflated sense of self-worth and self-importance.

Your humility is accepting the possibility – however minor - that someone has a greater ego than you.

The more people you meet, the more you like your dog.

You are a philanthropist – you pay your bills with other's charity.

You will have to change your faith since you no longer think you are God.

I have an inflated sense of self-worth and self-importance - continued.

You wife does not love you as much as you do.

You are so opinionated you make Rush Limbaugh look open-minded.

You are not much, but you are all that you think about.

I mask my pain in various ways such as anger, humor, or isolation.

When you called the suicide hot line in Bagdad, they just laughed and asked if you were wearing a vest.

When beating the dirt out of a rug, your ex-wife remembered it was your birthday and called.

Your anger has really got out of control; you now have a chip on both shoulders.

Irony scarred you—your mother called you "... son-of-a-bitch."

You frequently overdose on bitch pills.

Hollywood bought the rights to your life as an apocalypse-horror film.

You want to rewind your life like a country and western song sung backwards
- your dog comes home
- your wife never cheats on you
- your Momma doesn't die
- you never drank

I express negativity or aggression in indirect and passive ways.

Your most productive negotiating skill is settling.

Your best conflict resolution method is to stab your opponent in the back with the dagger of silence.

You tried to take the high road but lost the address.

The Bible says never to go to bed angry, so you stayed awake for three days.

So as to never offend anyone, you are always on the fence.

You are so negative; you look for a problem with every solution.

When given the choice between sticking with the rabble or joining the winners - you chose what you knew best ... *losers*.

I frighten people with my anger and belittling criticism.

The real miracle of Christmas - you made it through another year without killing your relatives.

You dislike your girlfriend's mother so much ... you married her daughter.

You can scream obscenities in 39 different languages.

You wanted to get back at you ex-husband so bad you put a bumper sticker on his car that read *Bikers Suck!*

I frighten people with my anger and belittling criticism - continued.

You wanted to get back at you ex-wife so bad you put a bumper sticker on her car that read *Please Help - I'm Horny!*

You really – REALLY wanted to get back at your ex - so bad - *you made up with him.*

The only therapist who will counsel you is a *Proctologist-Psychologist*. He only treats assholes.

With any disagreements, you escalate into a full-scale assault on why you are right.

I am attracted to the unavailability of others.

You are still in love with someone who went out for a beer and has not returned for 14 years.

I am attracted to the unavailability of others - continued.

You love talking to the back of a women's head.

Your psychic girlfriend left you before you met her.

There were no lifeguards watching your girlfriend's gene pool.

You struck out in the Little League so often your parents tried to trade you to another team.

When suffering with painful kidney stones, you asked your mother to take you to the hospital. She refused for she had "...a cake in the oven."

At the last single's dance, you tried to lasso a man with your umbilical cord.

I have difficulty attracting or maintaining intimate relationships.

Your girlfriend tells you she could miss you better if you were further away.

You drag others down to your idiotic level of thinking, and there you always beat them with experience.

The only reason to have a man in your life is your vibrator cannot fix a flat tire

When someone offers to give you an inch, you measure, declare it inadequate, and then demand the mile.

I have difficulty attracting or maintaining intimate relationships - continued.

Your definition of intimacy is buying your girlfriend a padded commode seat for Christmas.

Your holy wedlock turned into unholy deadlock.

In your family, there were too many freaks and not enough circuses.

When you came out of the womb, you shot the doctor the finger.

You enter the bar hoping to meet your future ex-husband.

I abandon others before they can abandon me.

You base your excessive wishes on equally extreme false hopes.

Your girlfriend would not leave you alone so you found someone who would.

You were out of your mind when you thought someone could possibly love you.

At your husband's funeral, you wore a black tennis dress.

When they elected you governor, you signed your own recall petition.

I abandon others before they can abandon me - continued.

> Others bring happiness upon arrival - you bring happiness when leaving.

> You are not selective in your prejudices - you hate everyone.

I need a compulsive personality, such as a workaholic, alcoholic, etc. to fulfill my sick abandonment needs.

> Your boyfriend is twisted, depraved, and rotten to the core ... just the way you like 'em.

> Your alcoholic boyfriend asked, "Will you marry me and be my mommy?"

> You smile and say ... *"Yes."*

> Your new girlfriend has more hang-ups than Ma Bell.

> You will date him again as soon as your skin stops crawling.

> Her character defects prevented your wife from getting a better husband.

> Your blind date played a prostitute in the Rocky Horror Picture.

> His perfected rudeness compliments your complete lack of decency.

I am terrified of abandonment and will do anything to hold on to a relationship.

Your marriage is like a dirty diaper, you'd change it but now ... *you're just used to it.*

You are more miserable without her than you were with her.

So many of your relationships crash and burn, you need an emotional airbag for your heart.

When your boyfriend was very depressed – like a deep dark well - you jumped in to save him.

You needed the FBI Hostage Negotiating Team to get your heart back.

When she said she was ending the marriage, you asked if you could go with her.

Every third day your marriage wasn't so bad.

Multigenerational

"... he punishes the children for the sin of the parents to the third and fourth generation."

—Numbers 14:18

Since man first discovered fermented grapes, the disease of alcoholism has held the humankind in a vice grip of despair. Over the years of evolution, addiction has mutated into many different and equally destructive addictions: drugs, gambling, sex, codependency, religion, sex and love, and the latest addiction – electronic addiction. Addiction has so permeated our culture that most people are affected directly or at least, tangentially.

The Joy Robbers presented in this book are not a complete set (see Appendix for the entire set). History does not record if they are the result of this disease or predated the fermentation of the grape. It matters not for these Joy Robbers are the coping skills that, through ignorance, we use to push away the intimacy and profound love only available in close relationships. When you identify with some of these *Joy Robbers*, challenge yourself - *are these working for me or am I pushing away what I want the most and then wondering why I am so lonely?*

These Joy Robbers have been passed down from one generation to the next and now have firmly landed in your lap – thud! The question is not why they are there. There is a much more important question, *what are you going to do about them*? Look at this question again and ask yourself, "What are **you** going to do about them?"

Today is the beginning of the rest of your life. You know the *Joy Robbers* have already cost you much happiness. Your response to this challenge has life-changing consequences. How you respond will affect the rest of your life, all the people you love for this generation and many to come. Your positive change is a powerful expression of love. What changes are you willing to make? What will you pass on?

WANTED
DEAD OR ALIVE
COMMAND/CONTROL
JOY ROBBER

Description: Takes control without permission, dictates the terms of another's life requiring others to strictly adhere to how she/he thinks they should live. Focuses on others with little or no regard to his/her own character defects.

CHAPTER FOUR

COMMAND/CONTROL JOY ROBBERS

Give yourself a score of 1-5 depending on your identity to the trait with 5 being the most.

I talk others into my reality – what they should think and feel.	
I do not need permission to dispense my valuable advice.	
Being needed is very important to me.	
I insist others meet my needs.	
I get others to agree by shame and blame tactics.	
Cooperating with others is not important to me.	
I manipulate others using rage, moral authority, or by being the victim.	
I believe people are incapable of taking care of themselves	
Others would not accept me if I were not sexual.	

I do not need permission to dispense my valuable advice.

Your friends know your advice is worthless, but they ask you anyway because they know how much you love to give it.

The only way you can keep from speaking your mind is to bite your tongue.

You have infinite wisdom to know exactly what others need to fix their problems ... but they never listen.

You are so good at pointing the finger at others you have become the poster child for bird dogs.

You make a list of those who need therapy, but your name is not on it.

Your King-Baby Syndrome requires the room to revolve around you.

When you speak, other people immediately visualize duct tape over your mouth

I manipulate others using rage, moral authority, or by being the victim.

Loud, obnoxious drunks make you feel embarrassed, and shame creating vivid memories of home.

You make your friends through violence.

You pray to God to lead you "...not into temptation..." knowing you are so successful at finding it on your own.

Your most effective coping skill is pushing away what you want the most.

Translating your "I could give a shit," means, "Please don't leave me."

For each action of others, you have a corresponding over-reaction.

You are so agitated you could wash an entire load of laundry in your sleep.

You muddle through life as a cleverly disguised adult.

Those who do not think like you are stupid. *Shout the dummies down!*

You bring downhill-mentality to uphill battles.

When one door closes, instead of looking for another, you either break it down or pick the lock.

You are an atheist who spends a lot of time being mad at God.

I believe people are incapable of taking care of themselves.

Your husband has a terrible sense of direction - he will not do anything you tell him.

Your best expression of friendship is slapping the stupidity out of your friends.

Your kids call your home *the Land of a Thousand Regulations*.

Your excessive pushiness is only exceeded by your over-developed need for control.

You bought your son a square baseball - so it would not roll away.

You are sure most of the world's problem can only be solved by you.

You are only happy when you have a roof over your head and a husband under your thumb.

I talk others into my reality – what to think and feel.

"Trust me" is what you tell your girlfriend when she says "no."

You faithfully attend church - to sharpen your judgmental skills.

Your attitude is not the problem ... it is other people's perception that causes trouble.

I talk others into my reality – what to think and feel - continued.

You see men as grapes you need to stomp and then properly age until they turn into something acceptable to have with dinner.

In the battle of tongues, you never can hold yours.

You are not a control freak just someone who needs to be in charge.

Your daughter-in-law does not heed your helpful advice as she is living with the results of your child-rearing.

Others would not accept me if I were not sexual.

Your firm resolve not to have sex dissolves when the doorbell rings.

When they built a new home for unwed mothers, you vowed to personally stock it.

When you enter a shady bar full of construction workers, there are many lewd and suggestive innuendos, but finally, they manage to shut you up.

As his mistress, you are a warm body between a mister and his mattress.

You go to work each morning from a different direction.

The threesome you planned was a disappointment – two did not show.

Others would not accept me if I were not sexual – continued.

A good time for you is when your conscience is guilty, but all other parts feel good.

The sex was so good - even the neighbors smoked cigarettes.

Sex takes so little time but causes you the greatest amount of trouble.

If sex were food, you would be morbidly obese.

Your sexual highlight of the year is when a dog sniffed your crotch.

Boys excite you when they whisper these magical little words in your ear, "I'll buy it for you."

You seek out bad relationships and are never disappointed.

I insist others meet my needs.

Your boyfriend has a screw loose, and you are determined to tighten it.

This life would be much easier if she would keep you in the life-style you would like to become accustomed.

You crash weddings for the cake and to be included in the photo-ops.

Since she concentrates on your every failing –you don't have to worry.

I insist others meet my needs - continued.

> You know you would have better choices if you eased off your martyr throttle.

> You buy self-help books -*all for your husband.*

> You don't just make mountains out of molehills you create entire mountain ranges.

I get others to agree by using shame and blame tactics.

> You look for others to co-sign your bullshit.

> The real reason you forgive your enemies is to mess with their heads.

> You seek controversy and are delighted when you are successful.

> Being self-employed, your boss is still an asshole.

> You don't hate anyone but read the obituaries with great relish.

> You are much better at fighting with your spouse now with all the practice.

> You pattern your life after your hero, Charlie Sheen.

> She said, "I'm cancelling my subscription – I'm tired of all your issues."

Cooperating with others is not important to you.

Your high school class voted you *Most Likely to Become a Terrorist*.

You even play tug-a-war with God.

The only control setting you have is ... out-of-control.

Your father is on death row, your mother runs a whorehouse, your sister is her best producer, and your brother robs banks. However, you have trouble telling your new love that you write joke books.

When you light the string on your tampon, everyone runs for cover

You wear green every day of the year *except* St. Patrick's Day

You got kicked out of your Tantric Yoga class for chanting *naughty words*.

You are as delicate as an AK-47.

The gift that keeps on giving is the pain you inflict on others.

You don't have time for patience.

Being needed is very important to you.

When she told you she had "...deep psychological problems" your heart fluttered with joy, thinking "This is the one!"

Being needed is very important to you - continued.

You prowl open AA meetings looking for your next reclamation project.

You are convinced only you can rescue needy men and stray cats.

The martyr-cross you so faithfully carry, you already willed to your daughter.

You describe your boyfriend as, "Way down deep, he's very shallow."

You donated your kidney so there will be someone who always needs you.

You are still tethered to your mother by your umbilical cord.

You are smart enough to check with his former girlfriends but discount their advice to run.

What you need is more backbone instead of your enlarged wishbone.

On every date, an Emotional M.A.S.H. unit follows you around to resuscitate you after the rejection.

Vanguard

If you did a survey in any Twelve-Step meeting asking whose parents or grandparents are in recovery, not many would raise their hands. Recovery is very new to the history of the human race – AA just started in the early thirties! That is one reason recovery is so difficult - *we are changing thousands of years of human history!*

You did not invent your dysfunction – *maybe perfected it* – you inherited your Joy Robbers from the big people in your life and they learned it from the big people in their lives down through many generations preceding you.

You are the vanguard of a new way of living. Through recovery, the changes you make allow you to change from "restless, irritated, and discontented" to becoming "happy, joyous, and free." This gift of recovery belongs to you. No one can take your contentment away! Once accepting this gift, peace and serenity can be yours. Only you can reject this magical gift now offered to you.

In addition, any positive changes you make send ripple effects around you to those you love today and for those in the third, fourth, and fifth generations, and your positive changes influence many more generations to come.

All you have to do it to change-*simple* ...
Not easy.

WANTED

DEAD OR ALIVE

LOW SELF WORTH

JOY ROBBER

Description: Has difficulty making decisions, judge themselves harshly, values other's opinion over own, does not feel okay or loveable, but successfully hides this from others, needs to be right and look good, difficultly identifying or asking for their needs, fails to set personal boundaries.

CHAPTER FIVE

LOW SELF-WORTH JOY ROBBERS

Give yourself a score of 1-5 depending on your identity to the trait with 5 being the most.

Decisions are often hard for me to make	
I am sure I am less than other people.	
Others are "normal" – I am not.	
I am not okay, good enough, or worthwhile.	
I try to make everything about me.	
I have an inflated sense of self-worth and self-importance.	
I have difficulty admitting a mistake.	
I need to be right and lie to look good.	
I have difficulty knowing what I need or want.	
I get feelings of guilt when I stand up for myself.	
I am okay - others are not okay.	
I am very controlling and/or hyper-responsible.	
I often procrastinate and show up late.	
I have trouble setting personal boundaries.	
I am very irresponsible.	
I am afraid of authority figures.	

Decisions are often hard for me to make.

Your rigidity often vacillates.

Your best ideas come from the depths of the sewer in your mind.

Your common sense is not very common.

You discount the wisdom earned from your scar tissue.

Two doors: one marked *Stairway to Heaven* and the other *Committee to Study How to Get to Heaven* - you choose the committee door!

Since the "pathway to hell is paved with good intentions," you keep your salvation intact with your bad intentions!

Indecision is the key to your flexibility.

You are positive about your ambiguity.

When considering the lesser of two evils, you choose both.

You realize you have to have a conscience before anyone can raise it.

I am sure I am less than other people.

You combined your poor spelling and very low self-esteem by printing on your designer tee shirt, *Looser!*

I am sure I am less than other people – continued.

You think that your inferiority complex is not as good as others.

You are a paranoid-optimist - good things are out to get you.

If you came from father's best sperm – what were his others like?

You woke up in the fraternity house wearing more clothes than when you passed out.

You act as your own prosecuting attorney, judge, jury and are proud of your 100% conviction rate.

When someone asks you to show them your best side, you realize you are sitting on it.

In your inadequacy, you have plenty for which to feel inferior.

A peeping Tom closed your window shades.

You fear your self-reliant will fail you.

You know that you could be a lot more worthless.

Others are "normal" – I am not.

It is not that you are ashamed, but only your pride is stuck in reverse.

Others are "normal" – I am not - continued.

> Someone put a "stop payment" on your reality check.
>
> You are such a pessimist even your blood type is negative.
>
> You tried to be you - but found being someone else safer.
>
> Being down on yourself is your most honest form of feedback.
>
> When you Google your own name, it came back ... *No Results.*
>
> Your self-esteem filed for bankruptcy.
>
> People call you Catfish - all mouth and no brains.
>
> You believe your imaginary friend dumped you.
>
> Someone peed in your gene pool.
>
> You are not crazy – insanity is normal for you.

I am not okay, good enough, or worthwhile.

> You think everyone hates you just because you are paranoid.
>
> You don't like to smile - it hurts your cheeks.
>
> Your own inner child tried to be adopted by someone else.
>
> Your greatest quality is running amuck.

I am not okay, good enough, or worthwhile - continued.

You have 289 Facebook friends but are dying from loneliness.

You tried to get in touch with your inner child, but he was not allowed to talk to strangers.

No matter how low your self-esteem, others think even less of you.

Your head is a scary place to be.

I try to make everything about me.

You received many sympathy cards after your failed suicide attempt.

You go to everyone else's funeral hoping they will come to yours.

When depressed, your shoulders stoop seeking pity from everyone but then get pissed from all their sympathy.

You are so hungry for attention; you would kill for a Nobel Peace Prize.

When you asked him, "Do you have to fall asleep when I talk?" He told you, "No, it is purely voluntary."

I have an inflated sense of self-worth and self-importance.

You look up into the night sky and see *your* face in the constellations.

I'm not much, but I am all that I think about.

You don't have an attitude – other people just don't have the personality to handle yours.

You are an egomaniac with a massive inferiority complex.

Your attitude is to keep your head held high and middle finger higher.

You are actually much greater than you think.

In the courtroom of your opinion, you have never lost a case.

You know you are not much but you are all that you think about.

Your magnetic personality does not have reverse polarity.

Rome "...wasn't built in a day ...", but then again, you were not in charge of that project.

There is always time to be humble on the rare occasion you could be wrong.

You make Sheldon Cooper on the Big Bang Theory TV show seems humble.

I have difficulty admitting a mistake.

You validate other people's inherent mistrust in humanity.

You think you just might be crazy but in your family - how would you know?

Others think you are lying, but to you, it's just alternative facts.

When you say, "I'm sorry," what you really think is, "I don't give a shit."

You always have to have the last word even when *arguing with yourself.*

You believe anyone who sees a therapist needs to get his head examined.

You are proud of your unblemished record of never saying, "I'm sorry."

You finally achieved the ultimate distinction of dishonesty when crowned, The *Wizard of Lies.*

You blame your relapse on attending too many AA meetings.

You already know the solution but your trouble is in applying it.

You are too afraid to admit your fears.

I need to be right and lie to look good.

> After you died, you refused to go to your eternal reward until you edit Saint Peter's book.
>
> You are so rigid you make a 2 x 4 look flexible.
>
> You can parley any criticism into a declaration of war.
>
> You graduated from Trump University with a Masters in Political Correctness.
>
> You drag others down to your level of idiotic, and there you beat them with experience.
>
> You have to have a keen brain to keep track of all your lies.
>
> You reject the free *Get Out of Hell Free* card. It might ruin your reputation.
>
> You can successfully argue with an empty room.

I have difficulty knowing what I need or want.

> In the court of your opinion, you are a rock-star.
>
> You brought your unmet needs to single's night at the grocery store expecting someone to fill your basket.
>
> You are too afraid to love yourself and terrified of others finding out.
>
> You are not in denial but immune to reality.

I have difficulty knowing what I need or want - continued.

Denial is your most treasured family value.

You were born an original but willing to die a copy.

You say, "Thank you," to automatic door openers.

Others love listening while you contradict yourself.

I get feelings of guilt when I stand up for myself.

You are drowning in shallow waters not knowing you can stand up.

When you finally got in touch with your inner child, he wet the bed.

On the island of misfit toys, you are the prize.

You wake up feeling guilty, even before you remember what you need to feel guilty for.

The only time you stood up for yourself, you hit your head on the ceiling of others' expectations.

You apologize when a drunk vomits on your shoes.

You are never hungry after eating your angry words.

I am okay - others are not okay.

Your nickname is Crabgrass ... you sprout up unexpectedly, ruin the atmosphere, and are *impossible to kill*.

I am okay - others are not okay - continued.

You are convinced your god can beat up his god.

You are so smart you are totally ignorant.

Your excuses are better than their requests.

Integrity to you is never admitting a mistake.

You think it was your spark that set off the Big Bang.

Looking at the billions of stars makes you realize how insignificant *they are*.

You filed a lawsuit against God.

Your boyfriend has serious gene pool issues.

Your co-workers are still alive only because it's illegal to shoot them, and you do not look good in orange.

Store mannequins have an easy life – people expect very little of them, their hearts are never broken, and never have head problems.

I am very controlling and/or hyper-responsible.

Your life has too many rules so you declared a new one to limit rules.

Your clear conscience comes from a bad memory.

I am very controlling and/or hyper-responsible - continued.

Others walk on eggshells around you anticipating your mood-change boomerang.

You spend many hours pointing out other's faults, but nobody appreciates all your hard work.

You are such a good husband; you let her go bowling last Thursday.

At an auction, you often bid against yourself.

You are not a control freak; you just insist on being in charge.

The word "no" is just the starting gun to begin your manipulation.

On your gravestone -*Here I am, see my tomb, now don't forget to clean your room.*

Your kids call you *Daddy Should-Ought*.

I look to others to provide my sense of safety.

You had a terrible custody fight with your Ex. You wife doesn't want you, and your mother will not take you back.

You turned in your resignation as an adult and now only accept the responsibilities of an 8-year-old.

I look to others to provide my sense of safety - continued.

> When you finally found the key to success, someone had changed the lock.
>
> You make your friends by butt dialing.
>
> You need a transfusion in order to bleed.

I often procrastinate and/or show up late.

> Doing nothing is hard work - your workday is never done.
>
> You make Charlie Brown look decisive.
>
> Your wishbone is much larger than your backbone.
>
> You love to hear the deafening thud of expectations as your deadlines thunders into the dustbin of the past.
>
> In the fog of indifference, you are unconcerned with the urgent call of tomorrow.
>
> You are not a procrastinator but rather... a *self-stopper*.
>
> You are much happier being late than those who are waiting.
>
> If you were punctual, there would be no one there to appreciate it.
>
> You are addicted to the, *I'm gonnas*.
>
> You make Beetle Bailey look motivated.

I have trouble setting personal boundaries.

You set a boundary once, or at least you thought you did.

Your excessive exuberance reminds people of a untrained puppy with *muddy paws*.

Your personal boundaries went on strike when your emotional check bounced.

You expect so little out of your relationships - you are never disappointed.

The border fence you were sitting on turned into a razor blade.

You confuse cuddling and holding someone down.

You tried to set strong boundaries, but Mexico would not pay for it.

Your wife learned to shoot because to you a restraining order is just a piece of paper.

You draw your personal boundary lines on an Etch-A-Sketch.

Once you hit your rock bottom, you found a trap door going down.

I am very irresponsible.

It is only your lack of money keeping you from expensive sins.

You run in circles from your problems to meet them head on.

The only reason you have not strayed from the straight and narrow is - you haven't had any good opportunities.

You have not yet trained your mouth not to say everything your brain is thinking.

Your assumptions can leap tall buildings in a single bound! Your resentments are more powerful than a locomotive!

> *Look up in the sky ... it's a bird ... it's a plane ... it's Super Jerk! Yes, its Super Jerk —a strange visitor in your own skin whose dysfunctions are far beyond those of moral men.*

Many people used to think you were worthless... *today they are certain.*

Your money always talks – it says "bye-bye."

You hate yourself too much to be happy.

Your intuition is the result of a lifetime of not thinking.

Your resentments are more powerful than a locomotive!

I am very irresponsible –continued.

>You are multi-talented - you can talk, walk, and piss people off – all at the same time.

>Your joy was waking up in a hospital bed instead of your mom crying over your grave.

>When in an ethical dilemma, you cannot lower your standards fast enough.

>Periodically you get reacquainted with the sheriff's office.

I am afraid of authority figures.

>You magnify other people's anger through the megaphone of your childhood.

>You hide from Big Bird on Sesame Street.

>You are terrified when Angry Bird plays on a cellphone.

>When Publisher Clearing House knocked on your door ... you hid.

>When someone is angry at you, you shudder like a dog crapping razor blades.

>If they would only change, you could finally get out from under the covers.

>When the umpire yelled "You're out!," you took it personally and left the ballpark.

The End

This book stops here - or does it? The humor will fade away hopefully leaving the memory of an enjoyable evening's read. However, your Joy Robbers will never end. They will continue to haunt all your relationships. They will continue to keep self-love out in the cold.

That's the bad news. Would you like to hear the good news? Of course you do - this is the real reason you read about your Joy Robbers —your painful reality. What you want is the opposite – the good news. *The Joy of Dysfunctional Families* presents the reality of what's been ailing you, all wrapped up in the numbing effect of tongue-in-cheek humor.

As monstrous as the Joy Robbers seem to be, there is a solution that is so simple most reject its difficult wisdom. To arrest your Joy Robbers, you need three things for your journey away from the unhappiness now controlling your serenity.

First, you need **awareness**. To connect to your character defects, you have to have guidance, and this book is your magical map. The Appendix greatly expands this necessary awareness.

Next - and probably the hardest part - **is to choose**. Just choose to put yourself in places of healing such as Twelve-Step meetings with Codependents Anonymous, Al-Anon, and/or Adult Children of Alcoholics. Therapy has also helped many.

The final ingredient necessary is **hope**. Allow yourself the necessary hope your life can change. This hope will allow you the set foot on the dark and walk the unseen path forward. The more you step out of your comfort zone into the darkness the more this hope turns in belief. Trust this process – just hope, take a step, and then enjoy increased trust as your hope turns into belief.

Know this – *your* joy is *your* birthright. Are you going to continue to choose unhappiness or accept what is already willed to you: *your* inheritance – *your* destiny – *your* happiness – *your* joy?

My Life Will Change ...
When I Change!

Appendix

The Appendix has three different but allied groups that are all involved in the recovery movement. They are Codependent Anonymous, Adult Children of Alcoholics, and Al-Anon.

Although all have an addiction of alcohol flavor, a person does not have to be raised in an alcoholic home to have some or all these traits. In fact, most people identify with many of these character defects, many of which are called Joy Robbers in this publication.

Co-Dependent Anonymous

Co-Dependents Anonymous is a twelve-step program for people who share a common desire to develop functional and healthy relationships.

Denial Patterns	
Codependents often...	**In Recovery...**
Have difficulty identifying what they are feeling.	I am aware of my feelings and identify them, often in the moment. I know the difference between my thoughts and feelings.
Minimize, alter, or deny how they truly feel.	I embrace my feelings; they are valid and important.
Perceive themselves as completely unselfish and dedicated to the well-being of others.	I know the difference between caring and caretaking. I recognize that taking care of others is often motivated by a need to benefit myself.
Lack empathy for the feelings and needs of others.	I am able to feel compassion for another's feelings and needs.
Label others with their negative traits.	I acknowledge that I may own the negative traits I often perceive in others.

Denial Patterns

Codependents often...	In Recovery...
Think they can take care of themselves without any help from others.	I acknowledge that I sometimes need the help of others.
Mask pain in various ways such as anger, humor, or isolation.	I am aware of my painful feelings and express them appropriately.
Express negativity or aggression in indirect and passive ways.	I am able to express my feelings openly, directly, and calmly.

Low Self-Esteem Patterns

Codependents often...	In Recovery...
Have difficulty making decisions.	I trust my ability to make effective decisions.
Judge what they think, say, or do harshly, as never good enough.	I accept myself as I am. I emphasize progress over perfection.
Are embarrassed to receive recognition, pra-ise, or gifts.	I feel appropriately worthy of the recognition, praise, or gifts I receive.
Value others' approval of their thinking, feelings, and behavior over their own.	I value the opinions of those I trust, without needing to gain their approval. I have confidence in myself.
Do not perceive themselves as lovable or worthwhile persons.	I recognize myself as being a lovable and valuable person.

Low Self-Esteem Patterns	
Codependents often...	**In Recovery...**
Seek recognition and praise to overcome feeling less than.	I seek my own approval first, and examine my motivations carefully when I seek approval from others.
Have difficulty admitting a mistake.	I continue to take my personal inventory, and when I am wrong, promptly admit it.
Need to appear to be right in the eyes of others and may even lie to look good.	I am honest with myself about my behaviors and motivations. I feel secure enough to admit mistakes to myself and others, and to hear their opinions, without feeling threatened.
Are unable to identify or ask for what they need and want.	I meet my own needs and wants when possible. I reach out for help when it's necessary and appropriate.
Look to others to provide their sense of safety.	With the help of my Higher Power, I create safety in my life.
Have difficulty getting started, meeting deadlines, and completing projects.	I avoid procrastination by meeting my responsibilities in a timely manner.
Have trouble setting healthy priorities and boundaries.	I am able to establish and uphold healthy priorities and boundaries in my life.

The Joy of Dysfunctional Families

Compliance Patterns	
Codependents often...	**In Recovery...**
Compromise their own values and integrity to avoid rejection or anger.	I am rooted in my own values, even if others don't agree or become angry.
Put aside their own interests in order to do what others want.	I consider my interests and feelings when asked to participate in another's plans.
Am hypervigilant regarding the feelings of others and take on those feelings.	I can separate my feelings from the feelings of others. I allow myself to experience my feelings, and others to be responsible for their feelings.
Accept sexual attention when they want love.	My sexuality is grounded in genuine intimacy and connection. When I need to feel loved, I express my heart's desires. I do not settle for sex without love.
Make decisions without regard to the consequences.	I ask my Higher Power for guidance, and consider possible consequences before I make decisions.
Give up their truth to gain the approval of others or to avoid change.	I stand in my truth and maintain my integrity, whether others approve or not, even if it means making difficult changes in my life.

Control Patterns

Codependents often...	In Recovery...
Believe people are incapable of taking care of themselves.	I realize that, with rare exceptions, other adults are capable of managing their own lives.
Attempt to convince others what to think, do, or feel.	I accept the thoughts, choices, and feelings of others, even though I may not be comfortable with them.
Freely offer advice and direction without being asked.	I give advice only when asked.
Become resentful when others decline their help or reject their advice.	I am content to see others take care of themselves.
Lavish gifts and favors on those they want to influence.	I carefully and honestly contemplate my motivations when preparing to give a gift.
Use sexual attention to gain approval and acceptance.	I embrace and celebrate my sexuality as evidence of my health and wholeness. I do not use it to gain the approval of others.
Have to feel needed in order to have a relationship with others.	I develop relationships with others based on equality, intimacy, and balance.

Control Patterns

Codependents often...	In Recovery...
Demand that their needs be met by others.	I find and use resources that meet my needs without making demands on others. I ask for help when I need it, without expectation.
Use charm and charisma to convince others of their capacity to be caring and compassionate.	I behave authentically with others, allowing my caring and compassionate qualities to emerge.
Refuse to cooperate, compromise, or negotiate.	I cooperate, compromise, and negotiate with others in a way that honors my integrity.
Adopt an attitude of indifference, helplessness, authority, or rage to manipulate outcomes.	I treat others with respect and consideration, and trust my Higher Power to meet my needs and desires.
Use recovery jargon in an attempt to control the behavior of others.	I use my recovery for my own growth and not to manipulate or control others.
Pretend to agree with others to get what they want.	My communication with others is authentic and truthful.

Avoidance Patterns

Codependents often...	In Recovery...
Allow addictions to people, places, and things to distract them from ach-ieving intimacy in relationships.	I practice my recovery to develop healthy and fulfilling relationships.
Use indirect or evasive communication to avoid conflict or confrontation.	I use direct and straightforward communication to resolve conflicts and deal appropriately with confrontations.
Diminish their capacity to have healthy relationships by declining to use the tools of recovery.	When I use the tools of recovery, I am able to develop and maintain healthy relationships of my choosing.
Suppress their feelings or needs to avoid feeling vulnerable.	I embrace my own vulnerability by trusting and honoring my feelings and needs.
Pull people toward them, but when others get close, push them away.	I welcome close relationships, while maintaining healthy boundaries.
Refuse to give up their self-will to avoid surrendering to a power greater than themselves.	I believe in and trust a power greater than myself. I willingly surrender my self-will to my Higher Power.

Avoidance Patterns	
Codependents often...	**In Recovery...**
Believe displays of emotion are a sign of weakness.	I honor my authentic emotions and share them when appropriate.
Withhold expressions of appreciation.	I freely engage in expressions of appreciation toward others.

"This was reproduced with the permission of Codependents Anonymous, Inc. Permission to reproduce this material does not mean that CoDA has reviewed or approved the contents of this book, or that CoDA necessarily agrees with the views expressed herein."
http://coda.org/

Adult Children of Alcoholics

The specific purpose for which this corporation is organized is to serve the Fellowship of Adult Children of Alcoholics [and otherwise Dysfunctional Families. It is in effect an agency created and now designated by that Fellowship to maintain services for those seeking, through Adult Children of Alcoholics [and otherwise Dysfunctional Families*], the means for arresting the emotional disease of family alcoholism. This is done by sharing information and experiences with one another and by applying to their own lives, in whole or in part, the Twelve steps which constitute the recovery program upon which Alcoholics Anonymous is founded.

Excerpted from the Adult Children of Alcoholics Article of Incorporation, January 12, 1987.**

The Laundry List – 14 Traits of an Adult Child of an Alcoholic

1. We became isolated and afraid of people and authority figures.
2. We became approval seekers and lost our identity in the process.
3. We are frightened by angry people and any personal criticism.
4. We either become alcoholics, marry them or both, or find another compulsive personality, such as a workaholic, to fulfill our sick abandonment needs.
5. We live life from the viewpoint of victims, and we are attracted by that weakness in our love and friendship relationships.
6. We have an overdeveloped sense of responsibility, and it is easier for us to be concerned with others rather than ourselves; this enables us not to look too closely at our own faults, etc.
7. We get guilt feelings when we stand up for ourselves instead of giving in to others.
8. We became addicted to excitement.
9. We confuse love and pity and tend to "love" people we can "pity" and "rescue."
10. We have "stuffed" our feelings from our traumatic childhoods and have lost the ability to feel or express our feelings because it hurts so much (Denial).

11. We judge ourselves harshly and have a very low sense of self-esteem.
12. We are dependent personalities who are terrified of abandonment and will do anything to hold on to a relationship in order not to experience painful abandonment feelings, which we received from living with sick people who were never there emotionally for us.
13. Alcoholism is a family disease; and we became para-alcoholics and took on the characteristics of that disease even though we did not pick up the drink.
14. Para-alcoholics are reactors rather than actors.

Tony A., 1978

Note: The Laundry List serves as the basis for **The Problem** statement.

The Flipside of The Laundry List

1. We move out of isolation and are not unrealistically afraid of other people, even authority figures.
2. We do not depend on others to tell us who we are.
3. We are not automatically frightened by angry people and no longer regard personal criticism as a threat.
4. We do not have a compulsive need to recreate abandonment.
5. We stop living life from the standpoint of victims and are not attracted by this trait in our important relationships.
6. We do not use enabling as a way to avoid looking at our own shortcomings.
7. We do not feel guilty when we stand up for ourselves.

8. We avoid emotional intoxication and choose workable relationships instead of constant upset.
9. We are able to distinguish love from pity and do not think "rescuing" people we "pity" is an act of love.
10. We come out of denial about our traumatic childhoods and regain the ability to feel and express our emotions.
11. We stop judging and condemning ourselves and discover a sense of self-worth.
12. We grow in independence and are no longer terrified of abandonment. We have interdependent relationships with healthy people, not dependent relationships with people who are emotionally unavailable.
13. The characteristics of alcoholism and para-alcoholism we have internalized are identified, acknowledged, and removed.
14. We are actors, not reactors.

The Other Laundry List

1. To cover our fear of people and our dread of isolation, we tragically become the very authority figures who frighten others and cause them to withdraw.
2. To avoid becoming enmeshed and entangled with other people and losing ourselves in the process, we become rigidly self-sufficient. We disdain the approval of others.
3. We frighten people with our anger and threat of belittling criticism.
4. We dominate others and abandon them before they can abandon us, or we avoid relationships with dependent

people altogether. To avoid being hurt, we isolate and dissociate and thereby abandon ourselves.

5. We live life from the standpoint of a victimizer and are attracted to people we can manipulate and control in our important relationships.
6. We are irresponsible and self-centered. Our inflated sense of self-worth and self-importance prevents us from seeing our deficiencies and shortcomings.
7. We make others feel guilty when they attempt to assert themselves.
8. We inhibit our fear by staying deadened and numb.
9. We hate people who "play" the victim and beg to be rescued.
10. We deny that we've been hurt and are suppressing our emotions by the dramatic expression of "pseudo" feelings.
11. To protect ourselves from self-punishment for failing to "save" the family, we project our self-hate onto others and punish them instead.
12. We "manage" the massive amount of deprivation we feel, coming from abandonment within the home, by quickly letting go of relationships that threaten our "independence" (not too close).
13. We refuse to admit we've been affected by family dysfunction or that there was dysfunction in the home or that we have internalized any of the family's destructive attitudes and behaviors.
14. We act as if we are nothing like the dependent people who raised us.

The Flipside of The Other Laundry List

1. We face and resolve our fear of people and our dread of isolation, and stop intimidating others with our power and position.
2. We realize the sanctuary we have built to protect the frightened and injured child within has become a prison, and we become willing to risk moving out of isolation.
3. With our renewed sense of self-worth and self-esteem, we realize it is no longer necessary to protect ourselves by intimidating others with contempt, ridicule, and anger.
4. We accept and comfort the isolated and hurt inner child we have abandoned and disavowed, and thereby, end the need to act out our fears of enmeshment and abandonment with other people.
5. Because we are whole and complete, we no longer try to control others through manipulation and force and bind them to us with fear, in order to avoid feeling isolated and alone.
6. Through our in-depth inventory, we discover our true identity as capable, worthwhile people. By asking to have our shortcomings removed, we are freed from the burden of inferiority and grandiosity.
7. We support and encourage others in their efforts to be assertive.
8. We uncover, acknowledge, and express our childhood fears and withdraw from emotional intoxication.

9. We have compassion for anyone who is trapped in the "drama triangle" and is desperately searching for a way out of insanity.
10. We accept that we were traumatized in childhood and lost the ability to feel. Using the Twelve-Steps as a program of recovery, we regain the ability to feel and remember and become whole human beings who are happy, joyous, and free.
11. In accepting we were powerless as children to "save" our family, we are able to release our self-hate and to stop punishing ourselves and others for not being enough.
12. By accepting and reuniting with the inner child, we are no longer threatened by intimacy, by the fear of being engulfed or made invisible.
13. By acknowledging the reality of family dysfunction, we no longer have to act as if nothing were wrong or keep denying that we are still unconsciously reacting to childhood harm and injury.
14. We stop denying and do something about our post-traumatic dependency on substances, people, places, and things to distort and avoid reality.

http://www.adultchildren.org/lit-laundry_list
"Laundry List" was originally written by Tony Allen in 1977.
copyright usage requested

Al-Anon

Al-Anon members are people, just like you, who are worried about someone with a drinking problem.

Did you grow up with a problem drinker?

These 20 questions are designed to help you decide whether you need Al-Anon Adult Children.

1. Do you constantly seek approval and affirmation?
2. Do you fail to recognize your accomplishments?
3. Do you fear criticism?
4. Do you overextend yourself?
5. Have you had problems with your own compulsive behavior?
6. Do you have a need for perfection?
7. Are you uneasy when your life is going smoothly, continually anticipating problems?
8. Do you feel more alive in the midst of a crisis?
9. Do you still feel responsible for others, as you did for the problem drinker (drug abuser) in your life?
10. Do you care for others easily, yet find it difficult to care for yourself?
11. Do you isolate yourself from other people?
12. Do you respond with fear to authority figures and angry people?

13. Do you feel that individuals and society in general are taking advantage of you?
14. Do you have trouble with intimate relationships?
15. Do you confuse pity with love, as you did with the problem drinker?
16. Do you attract and/or seek people who tend to be compulsive and abusive?
17. Do you cling to relationships because you are afraid of being alone?
18. Do you mistrust your own feelings and the feelings expressed by others?
19. Do you find it difficult to identify and express your emotions?
20. Do you think parental drinking may have affected you?

If you answered yes to some of these questions, Al-Anon Adult Children meetings may be able to help you.

> From Did You Grow Up with a Problem Drinker, copyright 1984, by Al-Anon Family Group Headquarters, Inc. Toll-free meeting information number, 888-4AL-ANON (888-425-2666) – website:, **http://www.al-anon.org/pdf/S69.pdf**

> *"If you want to make God laugh, tell him your plans."*
> From THE WISDOM OF THE ROOMS,"
> published by HCI 2019

Author's Note

Even children ***not*** raised in alcoholic homes often have many of these characteristics listed in the Appendix.

Suggested Reading

> *"Owning our story and loving ourselves through that process is the bravest thing we will ever do."*
> —Anonymous

7 Habits of Highly Effective People - Stephen R. Covey
Anger - Thich Nhat Hanh
Beyond the Relaxation Response - Hebert Benson. M.D.
Big Book of Alcoholics Anonymous - Bill Wilson
Codependency No More - Melody Beattie
Getting to Yes - William L Ury, Roger Fister, Bruce M. Patton
I'm Ok – You're Ok - Thomas A. Harros, M.D.
Just Listen - Mark Goulston
Learning to Love Yourself - Sharon Wegscheider-Cruse
Love - Leo Buscaglia
Man's Search for Meaning - Viktor E. Frankl
The Magic of Conflict - Thomas F. Crum
The Power of Now - Eckhart Tolle
The Way of the Wizard - Deepak Chopra
Understanding Co-Dependency - Sharon Wegscheider-Cruse
Wake UP! - Tom Owen-Towle
Wisdom of the Rooms - Mike Z.

> *"Books may well be the only true magic."*
> —Alice Hoffman

WANTED

IMPERSONATING AN AUTHOR

ENGLISH SMASHER

Description: Average height and build, brown hair with tints of grey, thinks he is humorous–jury is still out. Publishes self-help books about topics he personally needs to know about, has delusions of grandeur when describing himself as a writer, and is self-esteem challenged. Before recovery he scored high in the dysfunctional range of the quizzes included in this book.

Beware: He is armed and dangerous with insights– painfully obtained and 12-Steps wisdom. It is these qualities he uses as antidotes to life's Joy Robbers. Be careful, working a 12 Steps Program often leads into people who are happy, joyous, and free.

About the Author

David W. Earle, LPC is a mental counselor helping clients with anger management, substance abuse, compulsive gambling, eating disorders, anxiety, depression, and relationships. When he combines his Licensed Professional Counselor skills with his twenty-plus years of executive management experience, he conducts business coaching, a powerful matrix for transferring leadership skills. He is also a teacher, trainer, author, coach, and alternative dispute professional.

Earle earned a Master's of Science from Texas A&M and has held executive management positions in various fields including industrial construction, private investment banking, and corporate troubleshooting. He is now the president of the Earle Company, an organization dedicated to change.

He has published six books - three self-help books: *Love is Not Enough* (Changing Dysfunctional Family Habits), *Simple Communications for Complicated People* (Communication Made Simple), *What To Do While You Count To 10* (Management of Strong Emotions); and three-book trilogy of recovery poetry: *Professor of Pain* (A Lesson Before Living), *Iron Mask* (Peace Is Your Birthright), and *Red Roses 'n Pinstripes* (Despair to Meaning). He is writing a series of workbooks: *The Wisdom of the Twelve Steps*. These workbooks help recovery people work through the Twelve Steps. He has co-authored three books - two on leadership: *Leadership-Helping Others Succeed* and

Extreme Leadership, and a joke book entitled, *You Might Need a Therapist If...*

Earle has been on the panel as a mediator and/or arbitrator for various organizations such as U.S. Federal Court-Middle District, Equal Employment Opportunity Commission (EEOC), Financial Industry Regulator Authority (FINRA), Natural Futures Association (NFA), Federal Deposit Insurance Corporation (FDIC), and the Louisiana Supreme Court. He was on the faculty of the University of Phoenix for over 10 years.

His trademarked motto is *My Life Will Change... When I Change*™; he enjoys tennis, and he lives in Baton Rouge with his wife, Penny.

Request

The Joy of Dysfunctional Families is a work in progress. Nothing is perfect and this book will always need improvement. If you have suggestions, or improvements, I want to hear your thoughts. If you have a comment, positive or negative, or a good joke – contact me: earlecompany@cox.net.

Acknowledgement

Ms. Melissa Zraik accomplished the unenviable task of editing this book. Many people submitted humor to this collection often without realizing that I made a joke out what they said or did that would be forever enshrined in this his collection. Ms. Judith Gosse contributed by drawing the wonderful cartoons and creating front cover. Nick Caya did the final production formatting.

Penny, my bride of many years, has supported this writing with her own wit and encouragement when I felt discouraged. When deciding what joke to include and which one to exclude, her eye-rolled was my red flag – rewrite or discard.

Made in the USA
Monee, IL
07 October 2020